bullions & beyond

techniques and tips for mastering the crochet bullion stitch

by prudence mapstone

Published in Australia 2004
Publisher: Prudence Mapstone
Brisbane, Australia
Copyright © Prudence Mapstone

www.knotjustknitting.com
prudence@knotjustknitting.com

ISBN 0-9580443-1-7

Design & Photography by Dimity Mapstone

Models: Berni Chin & Kirsten Cameron

Printed by Kingswood Press
Brisbane, Australia

For everyone who has ever attempted but been frustrated by this amazing crochet stitch, it is my hope that the techniques outlined here will provide an easy method for mastering it. For those who have never come across this stitch before, I hope I can inspire you to add it to your crochet repertoire.

May you make bullions brilliantly!

Prudence

www.knotjustknitting.com

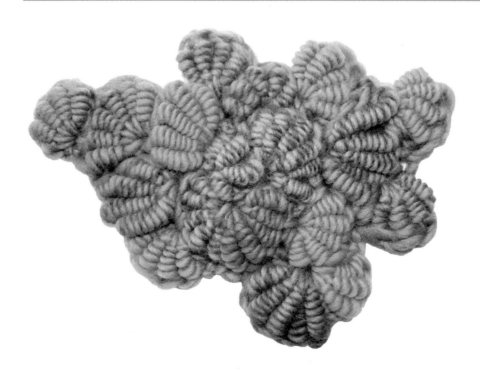

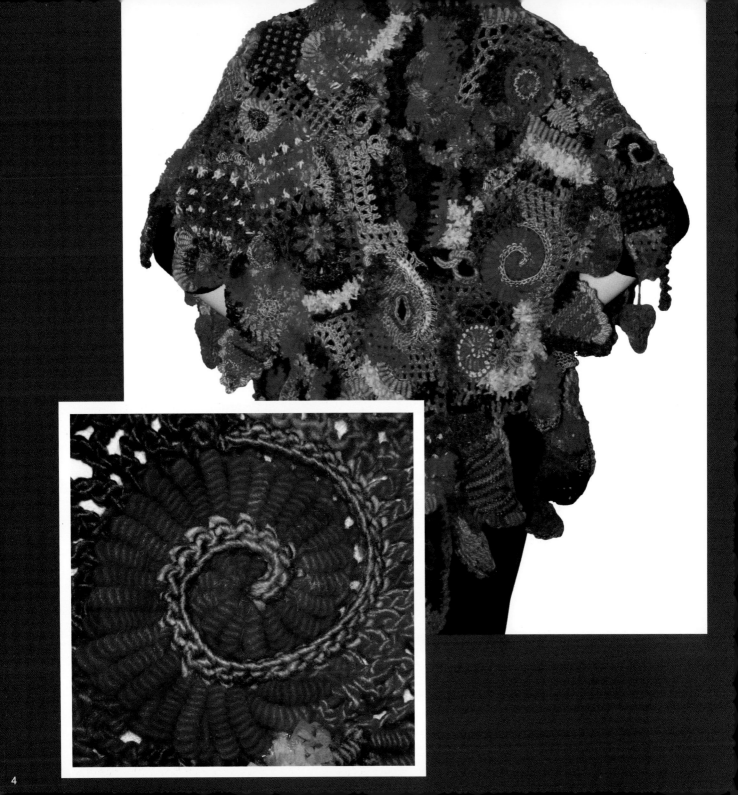

The elusive bullion

The crochet bullion stitch, also sometimes called the roll stitch, has probably been around for about 100 years. Even so, it is a relatively little-known stitch, possibly due to the fact that it has always been one of the most difficult crochet techniques to master.

It is similar in appearance to the bullions made in embroidery, where a number of strategically placed 'wrapped' stitches are often used to create small roses and buds. To achieve the stitch's distinctive effect it is necessary to twist the thread many times around the needle, and then draw the thread through all of the twists so that they will 'wrap' themselves around the sewing thread.

If you have ever tried to work embroidered bullions using a tapered sewing needle, you probably will have found that any variation in the width of the shaft of the needle can make it difficult to pull the thread through the stitch. Now imagine that, instead of a smooth needle, you are trying to pull through something that has a barb on the end, and you will see why creating the same effect using a crochet hook could become even more tricky.

Unlike embroidered bullions, the crocheted variety will require no backing fabric. The stitch can be worked into a length of crochet chain, or as a row of stitches made directly into the edge of a piece of crocheted or knitted fabric.

In many instances crochet bullions can be successfully substituted where other plain stitches are specified. For example, occassionally use a 5 or 6 wrap bullion instead of a treble (US: double crochet) to add an individual touch to a published pattern. When doing this, make the substitutions only in right side facing rows.

Used in various configurations you can also create many very unusual crochet motifs and designs, such as this striking shell shape, which was made by working progressively taller bullions into a 3 chain ring.

The addition of a few scattered bullions always seems to add an extra dimension to freeform crochet and knitting, and I find that it is invariably the bullion stitch motifs that are the most commented on in my freeform garments.

The few patterns that I have come across using this stitch generally intimate that the yarn needs to be pulled through all of the wraps in one fell swoop. For some people it may be possible to pull the hook through each of the yarn wraps swiftly and smoothly, but generally this is only after a lot of practice. To be able to make the stitch in this manner is not only dependent on how loosely or how evenly the yarn is wrapped, but also on the way both the hook and yarn wraps are held, the shape of the hook being used, and the very make up of the yarn itself.

Having demonstrated this stitch to so many people over the past few years, I have found that the more deliberate technique outlined on Page 11 will enable you to clearly see exactly how the stitch is progressing. Separating and holding the stitches open in the manner that is described will certainly mean that the yarn is less likely to get snagged in the process, and you also will find that the stitches are much less liable to fall off the hook. Even though it might seem as though it should be a slower process, in the long run this technique is probably just as fast, if not faster, for the majority of people.

Once you become more used to the stitch, you will probably find that you get into a rhythm when making your bullions, and your own comfortable method for separating the stitches and twisting the yarn through should soon develop.

It is not necessary to use a special tool to create this stitch, but sometimes the wraps may end up being made around parts of the hook that differ slightly in width. This often happens when the large number of wraps needed for a tall bullion mean that the yarn being twisted eventually goes over the thumb rest, where the size is marked on many brands of hooks. When this occurs, the completed bullion is less likely to be perfectly neat and tidy, although massaging the stitch into place once it is completed can sometimes help. A hook with a long, straight shaft will make this stitch easier to work, especially if you wish to create particularly long bullions, involving very many yarn wraps.

Smooth yarns make for more even bullions, and yarns that do not separate easily into individual plies are even less likely to snag when working the stitch. Single ply yarns with body are often the easiest yarns to use when making bullions, and they usually will produce tidier stitches. Sometimes chained or tightly spun yarns make things easier, too, although once you have mastered the stitch you will find that crocheted bullions can be made with virtually any yarn, thread, or hook, even if this sometimes results in varying degrees of neatness.

frontview

backview

To create the crocheted bullion, it is first necessary to make a number of wraps around the hook before placing the hook into the chain space or fabric. Any number of wraps can be made, but initially it is perhaps best not to try to make too many wraps when you are just learning the stitch. Four or five wraps will make quite substantial bullions, and with just a few wraps for your practice stitches you are much less likely to get your hook snagged on the way through, or have the yarn fall off your hook.

You may find it easier to work your first practice row of bullions directly onto a solid area of crochet or knitting rather than just into a length of crochet chain, as that will give you something more substantial to hold onto, and a firm foundation on which to work. Since the bullion is begun from the top, you will first need to make a couple of chain stitches to get your yarn into position before you start the wraps.

Technique

Choose a plain, smooth yarn of about the same weight as that used in the foundation piece you will be working onto, and a hook that approximately suits the thickness of the yarn selected. Join in the yarn and make 3 chain. If the piece of fabric you are working onto has a distinct front and back, make sure that you have the right side of the work facing towards you.

Evenly wind the yarn around the hook a number of times. For your first practice piece 4 or 5 wraps will be sufficient.

For the first bullion you could insert the hook into the same place as the chains, but then you will need to work along the row for the subsequent stitches. Place the hook into the fabric, yarn over hook, and draw the yarn through the fabric. Note that you will not be making any more yarn-overs until you reach the top of the bullion.

*Use the index finger on the hand that is holding the hook to pull the first wrap (i.e. the wrap that is next to the yarn-over and closest to the hooked end) up the shaft of the hook just slightly, gently rolling it towards you at the same time. This will open the loop up a little, and will make it appear somewhat looser, but it will not actually alter the tension.

Once the stitch is opened up, use the thumb and another finger on the other hand (i.e. the hand not holding the hook) to hold the loop down and open. Then turn the point of the hook downwards slightly, to ensure that the yarn-over that you are about to pull through is well trapped under the hook, and none of the strands get left behind.

Pull the hook just through the first loop - you might find that rolling your wrist slightly towards you as you do so will make this step easier. Now repeat this whole process (from * above) with each wrap in turn, until you have two loops left on the hook (i.e. the last wrap and the yarn-over that you have been pulling through). Keeping the point of the hook at the height of the almost completed bullion, yarn-over once again and take this yarn-over through the last two loops to finish the stitch.

Continue working bullions along the row, spacing them evenly.

If you turn the piece over you should see that you have a row of long, loose stitches at the back of the work if you have made all your final yarn-overs at the correct height. This is just the nature of the stitch, and is necessary to ensure that your bullion stitches stand tall and straight.

To create a piece similar to this, make a crochet chain the desired length, miss the first 2 chain, and work one double crochet (US: single crochet) into each of the chain to the end.   This row will be on the wrong side of the work. Chain 3, turn and work one bullion into each double crochet (US: single crochet). Chain 2, turn and work one row of double crochet (US: single crochet). Repeat these last 2 rows until your piece is the desired size.

Bullion rows

Again double crochet (US: single crochet) stitches were used for the wrong side facing rows in this piece, and bullions and trebles (US: double crochet) were alternated evenly across the right side facing rows.

In this piece double crochet (US: single crochet) stitches were again used for the wrong side facing rows, with 3 bullions and 3 trebles (US: double crochet) alternating for the right side facing rows, worked in a staggered pattern. Note the extra chains or stitches worked at the ends of some of the rows, to keep the edges even.

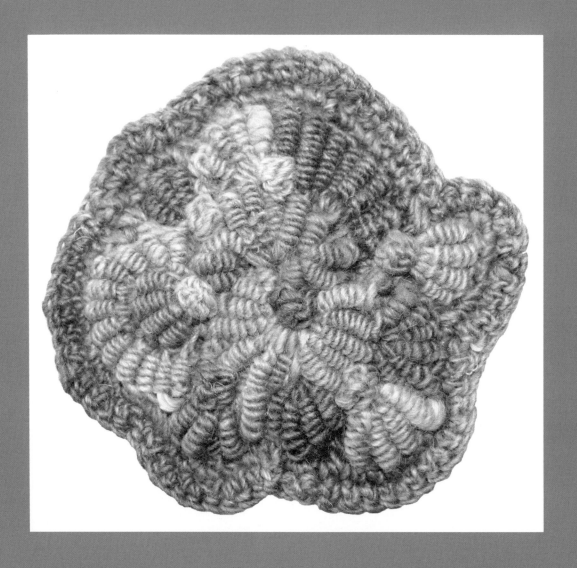

Bullion shells or clusters

With the right side of the work facing towards you, join a smooth yarn in at any desired position on your foundation piece. This time do not work any commencement chains, but immediately make the number of wraps you desire for the length of the completed bullion. Skip a number of stitches approximately equivalent to the finished height of the bullion, and insert your hook into the fabric. Yarn over hook, and complete the stitch as before. Your first bullion will lie flat against the fabric, but subsequent stitches will fan outwards to create the shell shape. Work more bullions into the same position, making only as many as it takes for the shell to reach back down to the fabric once again, and then join back into the fabric with a slip stitch.

In freeform work bullion clusters are a good way to fill in small v-shaped gaps on the edges of your patches. With the right side of the work facing towards you, join a smooth yarn in on one side of any right-angled or v-shaped gap at about the height that you think your bullion stitches will reach. The number of bullions made and the number of wraps required in these bullions will depend upon the size of the space to be filled. Make your bullions all into the same stitch at the bottom of the gap, working just enough to neatly fill the space. Note that it is generally better to work a stitch or two less rather than a few too many, to ensure that the work does not splay out and cause the other side of your patch to pop up. Join with a slip stitch to close, letting the height of the stitches determine the best position for joining.

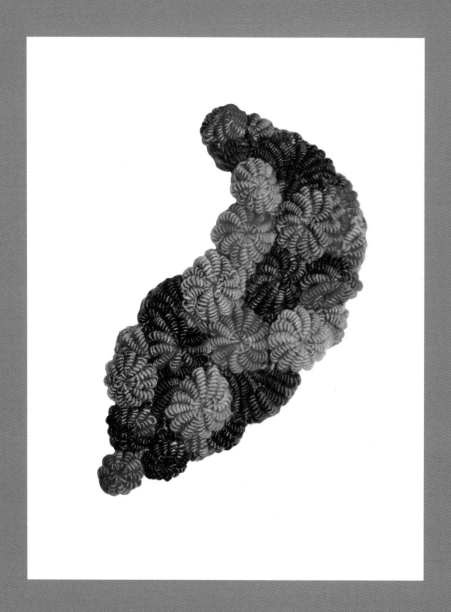

Bullion circles

Work 3 chain and join with a slip stitch to form a small ring, and then work approximately 3 more chain.

*Evenly wind the yarn a number of times around the shaft of the hook. The more chain worked, the taller each finished stitch, and the larger the completed circle. Insert the hook into the small ring, yarn over hook and draw the yarn-over through each of the loops until just two loops are left on the hook. Yarn over hook again, and draw through the remaining two loops. Repeat from * approximately 11 more times. Join with a slip stitch into the top of the 3 chain to close.

Bullion stitch is also very effective when worked around a small circle of fabric.

First create the centre section by joining 3 chain to form a small ring, working 3 more chain and then approximately 12 treble (US: 12 double crochet) into the ring, and joining with a slip stitch to close. If you wish to work this motif in two colours, finish off the first yarn now and join in a second. Make 3 chain, then work approximately two bullions into each of the stitches of the centre section, finishing with a slip stitch into the top of the 3 chain to close.

You can make many simple variations on bullion circle motifs, such as by alternating one bullion stitch and one treble stitch (US: one double crochet stitch) into the small ring until the motif is complete, rather than using only bullion stitches. In this motif, the 3 commencement chain will act as the first treble (US: double crochet).

Bullion circle variations

You could also add a second round as before, this time working one bullion stitch and one treble (US: one double crochet) into each of the stitches of the first round, rather than working two bullions into each stitch.

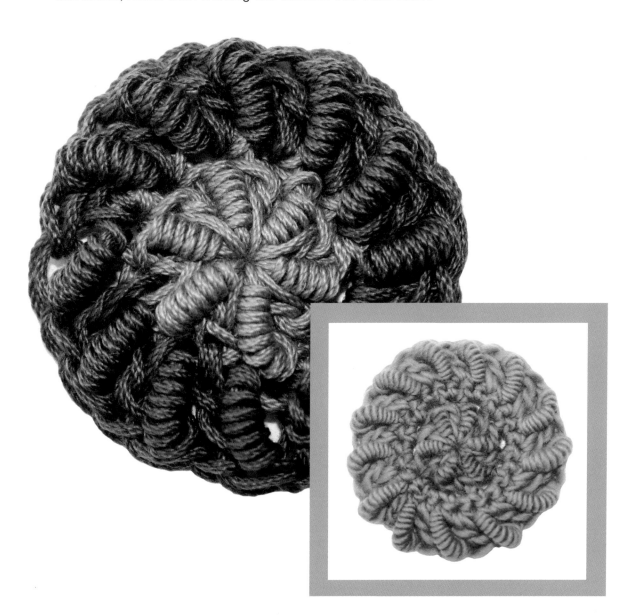

Bullion stitches also look very effective when worked around a small central oval shape. Firstly make a short chain, and then work a row of stitches of the desired height down one side of the chain. Work approximately three more stitches into the last chain and continue back down the other side to correspond, working a few extra stitches at the other end before joining with a slip stitch to close. Surround this small oval section with a continuous round of bullions, again being sure to work sufficient extra stitches as you turn the corners to prevent the motif puckering.

Experiment further by adding different height bullions around a central chain or other shapes.

Bullion height change ideas

Bullion spirals in two colours

Choose two yarns of approximately the same weight in contrasting colours. Make sure that Colour 2 is a smooth yarn that is suitable for bullions.

Using Colour 1, make 3 chain and join with a slip stitch to form a small ring. Make 3 more chain, and work approximately 10 treble (US: 10 double crochet) into the ring. Pull up a long loop by loosening the loop on the hook, and remove the hook. This will stop the stitches from unravelling as you work the other colour. Join Colour 2 into the centre of the small ring, make 3 chain, and work one or two bullion stitches into the ring. Still using Colour 2, begin to spiral up each of the 3 ch and then into the trebles (US: double crochet stitches) that were made with Colour 1, working 2 bullions into each stitch of the previous round. When you run out of stitches into which you can work, again pull up a long loop and remove the hook. Then go back to working with the previous colour once again. Continue in this manner until your motif is the desired size, being sure to only make approximately 12 increases in each completed circuit of the motif if you wish it to continue to lie flat (i.e. you will need to increase into every stitch for the second round, but only into every second stitch in the third round).

Many variations can be made to these Bullion Spirals, by changing any of the following:

· Substitute double crochet (US: single crochet) or half trebles (US: half double crochet) for the treble (US: double crochet) stitches

· Make more or less wraps for all of the bullions

· Gradually increase the number of wraps made for the bullions as the spiral progresses outwards (e.g. make 3 wraps for, say, the first 4 bullions, 4 wraps for the next 4, 5 for the next 4, and so on until the motif is the desired size).

Rows using more than one colour

Changing colour along or around a row of bullions is a great way to get the stitches to stand out even more. When working any crochet stitches with more than one colour, always work the final yarn-over of the previous stitch with the new yarn that is about to be used, to prevent the previous colour carrying across on the top of the new stitch to be worked.

As you can see, many new design possibilities could become available to you once you incorporate the bullion stitch into your crocheting.

Whether it be in freeform work or for more traditional crochet, I hope that some of these ideas and techniques inspire you to create your own textile masterpieces.

Happy crocheting!

For more information on Prudence's work,
visit her website at -
www.knotjustknitting.com

To learn more about Freeform methods for
crochet and knitting, read:

Freeform: Serendipitous Design
Techniques for Knitting and Crochet
by Prudence Mapstone
ISBN 0-9580443-0-9

Notes

Notes

Notes